Kylie Jean

Summer Camp Craft Queen

by Marne Ventura and Marci Peschke
illustrated by Tuesday Mourning

PICTURE WINDOW BOOKS
a capstone imprint

Editor: Shelly Lyons
Designer: Tracy Davies McCabe
Craft Project Creator: Marcy Morin
Photo Stylist: Sarah Schuette
Art Director: Nathan Gassman
Production Specialist: Laura Manthe

Picture Window Books
are published by Capstone,
1710 Roe Crest Drive,
North Mankato, Minnesota 56003
www.capstonepub.com

Library of Congress Cataloging-in-Publication Data
Ventura, Marne and Marci Peschke.
Kylie Jean summer camp craft queen /
by Marne Ventura and Marci Peschke.
pages cm — (Nonfiction picture books.
Kylie Jean craft queen.)
Audience: Age 7-9.
Audience: Grades K to 3.
Summary: "Introduces crafts related to the book Kylie
Jean Summer Camp Queen, by Marci Peschke"—
Provided by publisher.
Includes bibliographical references and index.
ISBN 978-1-4795-2193-7 (library binding)
1. Handicraft—Juvenile literature. 2. Camps—Juvenile
literature. 3. Summer—Juvenile literature. I. Peschke,
M. (Marci). Summer
camp queen. II. Title. III. Title: Summer camp
craft queen.
 TT160.V45 2014
745.5—dc23   2013032214

Photo Credits
All photos by Capstone Studio/Karon Dubke
Design elements: Shutterstock

Printed in the United States of America in Brainerd, Minnesota.
092013   007770BANGS14

Table of Contents

Introduction **4**

Tools and Tips **5**

Heavenly Scented Flowers **6**

Pretty Pink Checkers Set **8**

Flitter Flutter Butterfly **10**

Pretty Pop-Up Card **12**

Future Queen Tiara **14**

Best Friends Forever Bracelet **16**

Beautiful Butterfly T-Shirt **18**

Pretty Princess Plaque **20**

Rickrack Tic-Tac-Toe **22**

Lovely Leaf Stamp Banner **24**

Nutshell Picture Frame **26**

Country Girl Nature Wall Hanging **28**

Spirit Stick **30**

Read More **32**

Internet Sites **32**

Dear Crafters,

At Camp Mariposa we say, "Flitter, flutter, flee, you can't catch me! I create, inspire, and achieve. I'm a Mariposa girl!"

When you make all of my fun and easy camp crafts, you'll feel just like a Mariposa girl. Some of these projects are games to play, things to wear, and nature crafts. Of course, my favorite crafts are the sparkly tiara and checkers.

Remember to show your camp spirit by sharing your supplies. Happiness is crafting, so grab a friend, and get started. You'll love these crafts more than s'mores!

Your friend,

Kylie Jean

TOOLS NEEDED

- cellophane tape
- fabric glue
- foam paintbrush
- glue sticks
- hot glue gun
- markers
- paintbrush

- paper clips
- pencil
- pruning shears
- plastic lid
- pruning shears
- ruler
- scissors

- spray glue
- tapestry needle
- tempera or acrylic paint
- watercolor paints
- white glue

TIPS

- Before starting a project, read all of the steps and gather all of the supplies needed.
- Work on newspaper or paper towels.
- Ask an adult to help you use a hot glue gun and sharp tools.
- Give glue and paint plenty of time to dry before handling a project.

Heavenly Scented Flowers

Y'all are going to love making these colorful flowers! I'm going to make them for Momma, Granny, and Nànny. They remind me of Miss Clarabelle's yard. That makes me homesick!

You will need:
- 4, 20x26-inch (51x66-centimeter) tissue paper sheets (different colors)
- 3-inch (7.6-cm) plastic lid
- pencil
- scissors
- 2 paper clips
- chenille stems
- vase
- thin ribbon
- cologne, perfume, or air freshener

1. Fold the tissue paper in half five times. First fold top to bottom. Next fold side to side.

2. Use the plastic lid to draw a circle on the tissue paper.

3. Hold the layers of tissue together with one hand. Cut around the circle with the other.

4. Layer five or six circles together, and clamp each side with a paper clip. Near the center, poke the stem through to the other side. Then poke it again so it comes back up on the same side, the way you push a needle in and out to sew.

5. Twist the short end of the chenille stem around the top of the long end. This will hold the layers of paper together. Remove the paper clips.

6. To make the petals, hold the stem just under the paper. Starting with the top layer of paper, pinch the circle upward near the center.

7. Scrunch the next layer of tissue upward to make more petals. Continue until all the layers look like petals. Repeat steps 1–7 to make more flowers.

8. Arrange your flowers in a vase. Decorate with a pretty ribbon bow.

9. Spray with your favorite cologne or perfume for a heavenly scent!

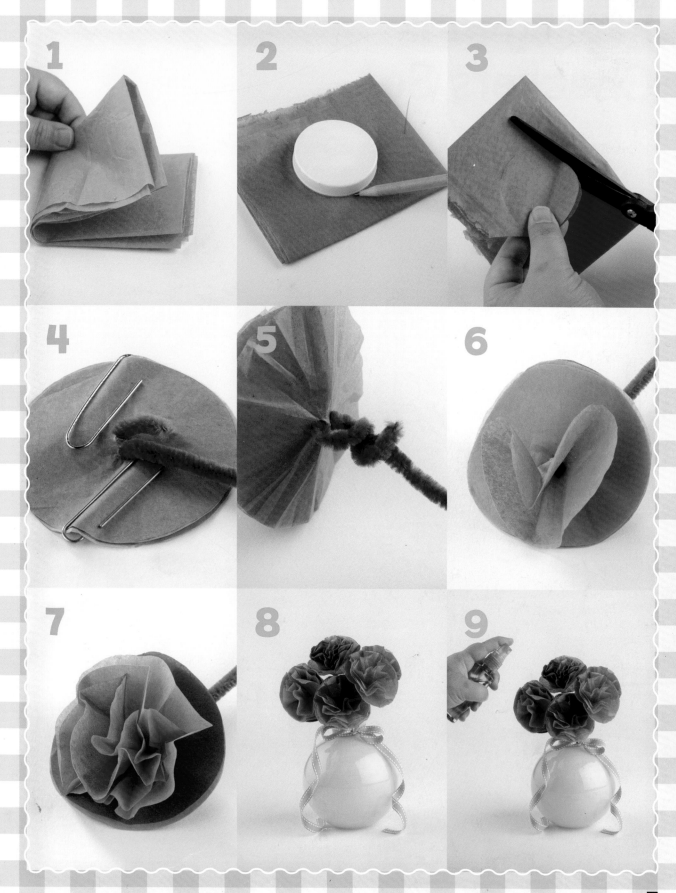

Pretty Pink Checkers Set

Pink checkers are so divine! Y'all know pink is my best color. I'm going to make the rest of my checkers silver. I love playing checkers and saying "Crown me!"

You will need:

- 12x12-inch (30x30-cm) piece of pink poster board
- ruler
- pencil
- scissors
- 12x12-inch (30x30-cm) piece of purple felt
- glue stick
- 24 plastic bottle caps
- white glue
- glitter

1. Use the ruler and pencil to draw a grid on the poster board. There should be 8 rows across and 8 rows down. Make each square 1 ½ inches (3.8 cm) by 1 ½ inches (3.8 cm).

2. Draw a 1 ½-inch (3.8-cm) square on the felt. Cut out. Repeat until you have 32 squares.

3. Spread glue over a corner square on the poster board. Place a felt square onto the glued square.

4. Glue a felt square on the next kitty-corner square of the poster board. Continue in a checkerboard pattern.

5. Use plastic bottle caps for checker pieces. You will need two sets of 12. Spread white glue on the top of each bottle cap, and sprinkle with glitter. Make each set a different color. Let dry.

Flitter Flutter Butterfly

At Camp Mariposa, we flitter, flutter, flee, just like butterflies!
I made my very own butterfly to set on my windowsill at
home. It reminds me of Camp Mariposa, and even my dog,
Ugly Brother, likes it!

You will need:

- coffee filters
- paper towels
- watercolor paints
- paintbrush
- water
- ruler
- chenille stems

optional:
- stick-on rhinestones

1. Flatten a coffee filter on a paper towel.

2. Paint the coffee filter with your favorite colors. To make the colors run together, brush water on the filter, and then paint.

3. When the paint is dry, fold the coffee filter like a fan. Starting on one side, fold over 1 inch (2.5 cm). Then fold 1 inch (2.5 cm) in the opposite direction. Continue until the whole filter is pleated like an accordion.

4. Bend the chenille stem in half and twist a few times near the bend. This is the butterfly's body.

5. Place the center of the folded filter between the two chenille stem ends just above the body. Twist the stem once or twice above the filter.

6. Open out the sides of the filter to make wings, and bend the ends of the stem into antennae.

Optional: Add stick-on rhinestones to the body and the tips of the antennae.

Pretty Pop-Up Card

Make this fancy letter paper, and write to your favorite person. Mine has four legs! If you guessed Ugly Brother, you're right. P.S. Write your momma a letter too.

You will need:
- blank card and envelope
- ruler
- fine-tipped markers
- 2 pieces of different colored construction paper
- scissors
- glue stick
- white glue or tape

1. Use a ruler and marker to draw a border on the outside of the blank card. Decorate with markers.

2. Cut a rectangle of construction paper that's about ½ inch (1.3 cm) smaller than the inside of the card. Fold it in half to match the fold of the white card.

3. To make a pop-up tab, measure 1 inch (2.5 cm) on the fold from the edge of the pink card. Cut a 1-inch (2.5-cm) slice from the fold in the card. Cut another 1-inch (2.5-cm) slice 1 inch (2.5 cm) away from the first slice. Repeat on the other side of the card. Then push in the tabs so they fold in the opposite direction of the crease.

4. Cut a moon and a heart shape from construction paper. Start with two circles that are each 3 inches (7.6 cm) in diameter.

5. Use the glue stick to attach the pop-up card to the inside of the blank card. Then write your message with a fine-tipped marker along the bottom of the construction paper.

6. Use white glue or tape to attach the heart and moon to the pop-up tabs.

Future Queen Tiara

This tiara will make you feel just like royalty. I love a crown with extra silver glitter. When you're done, look in the mirror and practice the beauty queen wave!

You will need:

- wagon wheel pasta
- paper towels
- spray glue
- glitter
- headband
- small box
- hot glue gun

1. Place 10 pieces of wagon wheel pasta on paper towels. Spray with glue. Sprinkle with glitter. Let dry.

2. Turn over all of the pasta pieces. Spray with glue, and sprinkle with glitter. Let dry.

3. Place the headband on a box so it will stand up.

4. Use a glue gun to attach a row of seven wagon wheels to the top of the headband. Use lots of glue, and give it plenty of time to dry.

5. When the glue is dry, add a second row of two wagon wheels. Let dry.

6. When dry, add the final wagon wheel to the top. Let dry.

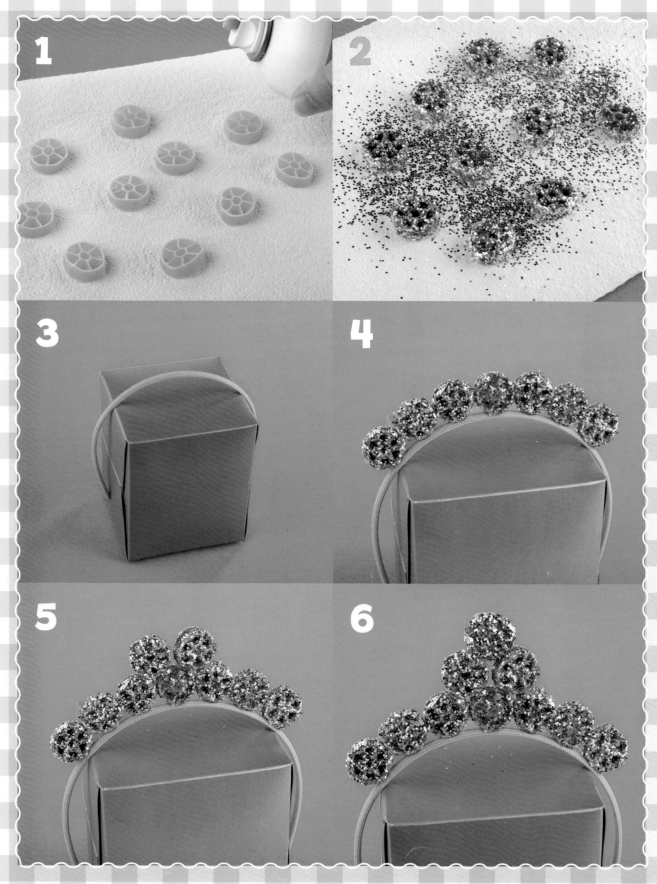

Best Friends Forever Bracelet

I always make pink friendship bracelets, and you can too. You may have lots of friends to make cute bracelets for!

You will need:

- embroidery floss
- ruler
- scissors
- cellophane tape
- bead

1. Choose three colors of embroidery floss. You will need two full strands of each color. Don't separate the threads. Cut 1 yard (.9 meter) of each color.

2. Put the six strands together and fold them in half. With an adult's permission, tape the center to a table or desk.

3. Form a loop that's big enough to fit over your bead. Tie a knot to secure the loop.

4. Separate the colors so you have three groups. Each group is four strands of one color.

5. Braid the three colors until the bracelet is long enough to go around your wrist.

6. Tie all the strands into one knot.

7. Wrap a piece of tape around the end of the strands to look like the end of a shoelace. Thread a bead onto the end.

8. Cut off the tape, and tie another knot to hold the bead in place. Trim the edges to make a pretty fringe.

9. Put the bead through the loop to form a bracelet.

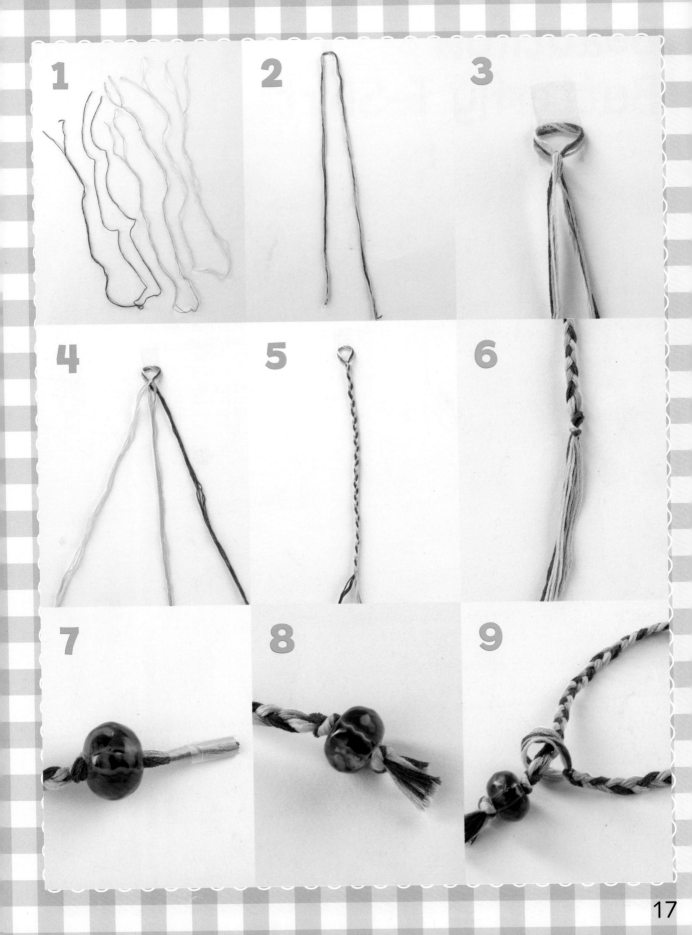

Beautiful Butterfly T-Shirt

This is a super simple butterfly T-shirt. It's so easy to make that I'm going to have time to put flowers on mine. Butterflies love flowers. Camping clothes are kinda cool!

You will need:

- 6 to 8, 12x12-inch (30x30-cm) sheets of different colored felt
- scissors
- ruler
- fabric glue
- T-shirt

optional:
- stick-on rhinestones

1. For each shape you want to make, cut a 2-inch (5-cm) circle from felt.

2. For a butterfly, fold the circle in half and cut a large and small wing. The fold is the center of the butterfly.

3. For a heart, fold the circle in half and cut half of a heart. The fold is the center of the heart.

4. For a flower, cut five triangles from the edge of the circle toward the center. This will make five petals.

5. Cut leaves from green felt.

6. Glue the felt shapes to the T-shirt with fabric glue. Let dry.

Optional: Add stick-on rhinestones to the shapes.

You can download a free template for this craft at capstonekids.com.

Pretty Princess Plaque

Princesses are beautiful and so are plaques! When you make your plaque you can even use pink pearls. I put "KJ" on mine, for Kylie Jean, of course!

You will need:

- wooden oval plaque
- scrapbook paper
- pencil
- scissors
- acrylic paint
- small paintbrush
- decoupage
- foam brush
- craft cord
- hot glue gun
- ribbon
- stick-on rhinestones
- bow accents

optional:
- adhesive hook

1. Trace the shape of the wooden plaque onto the back of the scrapbook paper. Cut out.

2. Paint the edges of the wooden piece. Let dry.

3. Apply a layer of decoupage on the wood piece, as well as on the back of the paper shape.

4. Place the back of the paper shape onto the front of the wooden plaque. Smooth out with fingers. Apply a second coat of decoupage on top for a finished look. Let dry.

5. Create your initials from craft cord. Tie knots at the ends of each letter.

6. Hot glue the letters to the front of the plaque.

7. Hot glue both ends of the ribbon to the back of the plaque near the top.

8. Use rhinestones and bow accents to decorate the plaque.

Optional: Use an adhesive hook to hang the plaque on your bedroom door.

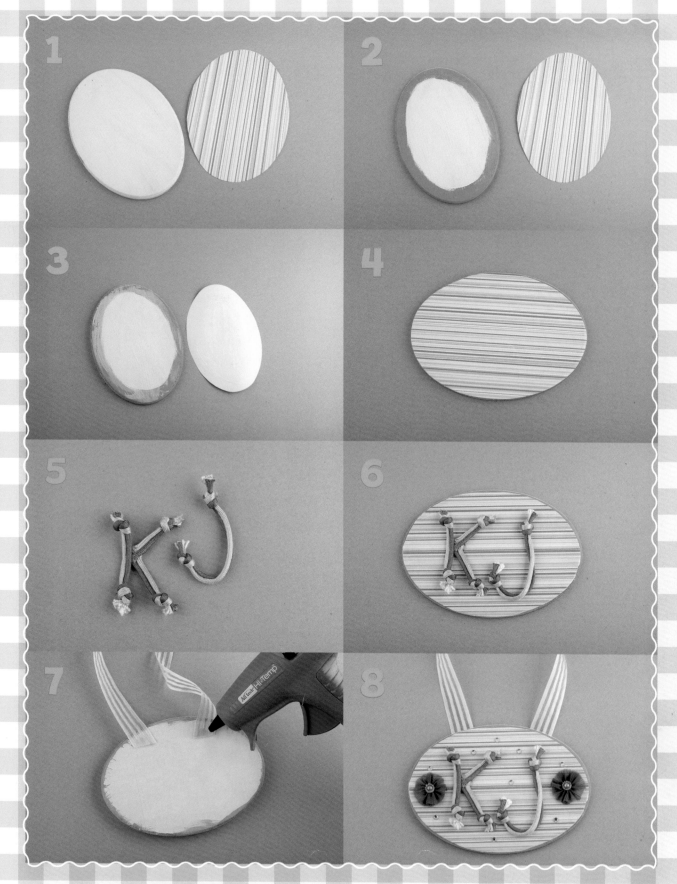

Rickrack Tic-Tac-Toe

Tic-tac-toe is a traveling game. You can play it anywhere. I just love the "X"s and "O"s because they're like hugs and kisses.

You will need:

- 3, 12x12-inch (30x30-cm) pieces of different colored felt
- ruler
- scissors
- marker
- rickrack
- fabric glue
- 2-inch (5-cm) plastic lid
- plastic zip-tight bag

optional:
- stick-on rhinestones

1. Cut a 9-inch (23-cm) by 9-inch (23-cm) square of felt.

2. Mark a 3-inch (7.6-cm) square grid using a marker and ruler.

3. Cut four 10-inch (25-cm) strips of rickrack.

4. One at a time, squirt glue along the rickrack and place it along the lines on the felt. A bit of rickrack will hang over each edge. Let it dry completely.

5. Trim the rickrack even with the edges of the felt.

6. Use a plastic lid or cup with a 2-inch (5-cm) diameter to draw five circles on felt. Cut out. These are your "O"s.

7. Cut out five more circles, just as you did in step 6, but from a different color of felt. From each circle, cut out an "X" shape.

8. Pack this game in a plastic zip-tight bag, and you can take it anywhere!

Optional: Use stick-on rhinestones to decorate your board.

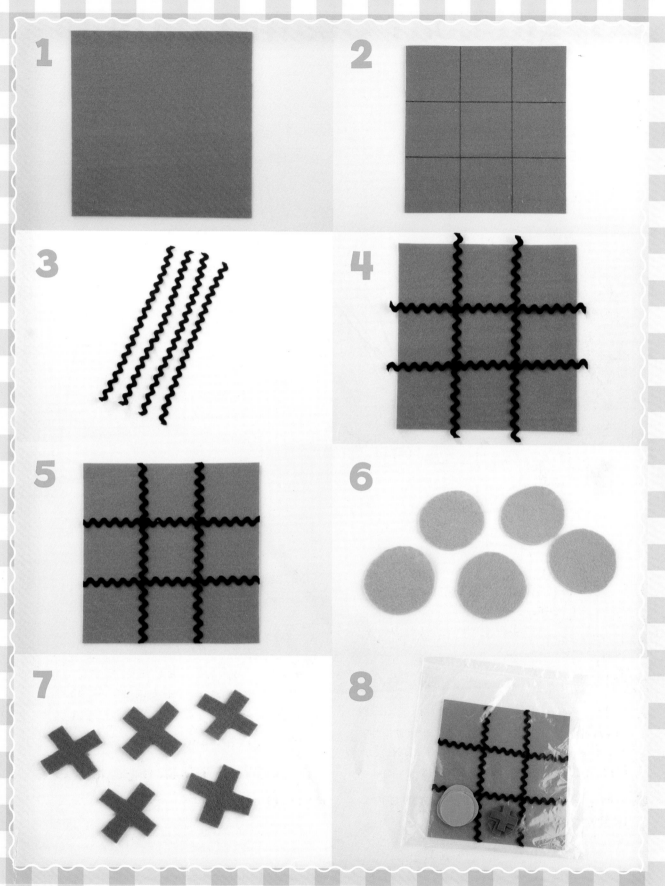

1

2

3

4

5

6

7

8

Lovely Leaf Stamp Banner

I started with a nature walk and ended with a craft project. My dog, Ugly Brother, got in the paint, and my leaf prints ended up looking like paw prints!

You will need:

- card stock
- ruler
- scissors
- pencil
- brown paper grocery bag
- paper towels
- tempera or acrylic paint
- leaves
- paintbrush
- yarn or string
- cellophane tape
- beads

optional:
- glitter glue
- stick-on rhinestones

1. Cut a 5½-inch (14-cm) square from card stock. Using a ruler, draw a triangle. Cut out. This is your triangle pattern.

2. Use the pattern to trace seven triangles onto the grocery bag. Cut out.

3. On a paper towel, brush one leaf with paint.

4. Lay the painted side of the leaf on one of the triangles. Cover it with a paper towel and press it gently so the paint goes onto the triangle. Peel off the paper towel and the leaf.

5. Repeat step 4 with all of the leaves, until all triangles are stamped. Use different colors, and put the leaves in different positions.

6. When the paint is dry, fold the bottom of each triangle over about ½-inch (1.3 cm).

7. Cut about 5 feet (1.5 meters) of yarn or string. Leaving a 1-foot (31-cm) end, tape the folded bottom of a triangle over the string.

8. On the other end of the string, wrap tape to make the end of the string stiff like a shoelace.

9. String a few beads on before taping the next triangle onto the string. Continue in this pattern until the last triangle has been added.

Optional: Use glitter glue and stick-on rhinestones to make your leaves sparkle.

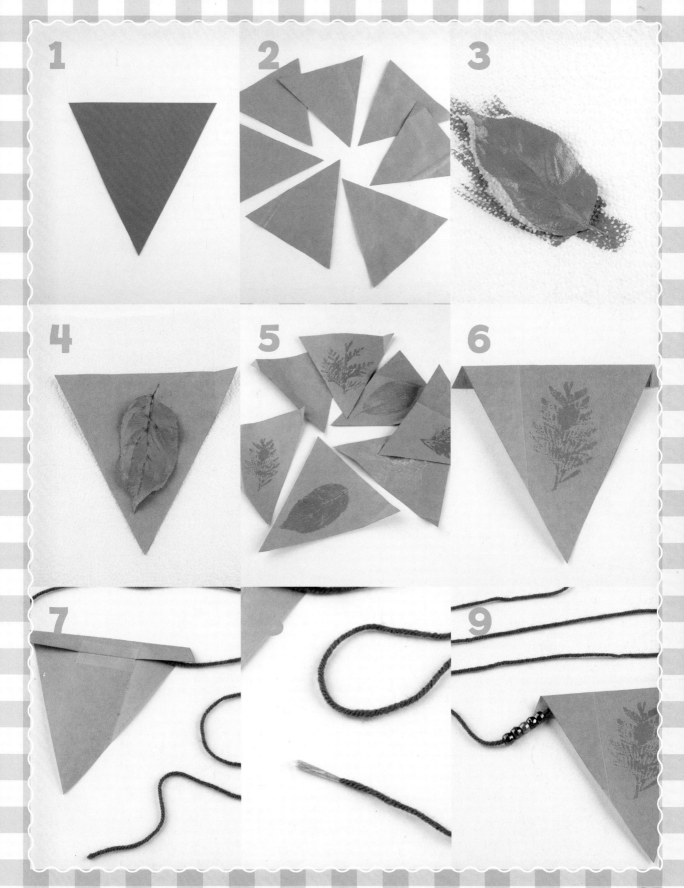

Nutshell Picture Frame

This nutshell frame is so cute! You get to paint and glue when you make it. I'm going to put a photo of my horse, Star, in mine.

You will need:

- unbroken nutshell halves
- acrylic paint
- paintbrush
- paper towels
- glue stick
- picture (photo or artwork)
- poster board
- ruler
- scissors
- white glue
- marker
- cellophane tape

optional:
- ribbon
- stick-on rhinestones
- pink pearls

1. Paint about 24 nutshell halves. Hold the shell on the tip of your finger to paint. Place on paper towels to dry.

2. Use the glue stick to cover the back of your picture with glue. Place in the center of the poster board.

3. Trim the poster board, leaving a 2-inch (5-cm) border around the picture.

4. Squirt white glue along the edges of the dry shells. Then arrange them like leaves on a vine around the border of the poster board. Let dry.

5. Use a marker to draw the vine that connects all the leaves.

6. To make a stand for your frame, cut a strip of poster board that is 2 inches (5 cm) wide and about 12 inches (30 cm) long. Fold it into a triangle and tape it closed. Attach it to the back of the frame with tape.

Optional: Use ribbon, stick-on rhinestones, and pink pearls to decorate your frame.

Country Girl Nature Wall Hanging

This nature wall hanging reminds me of my Earth Day project. You can even add glitter to make your pinecones sparkle. I like nature!

You will need:

- pruning shears
- smooth twig
- pink acrylic paint
- paintbrush
- colorful string or embroidery floss
- scissors
- ruler
- hot glue gun
- pinecones and acorns

optional:
- white glue
- glitter

1. Go on a nature hunt for a twig, pinecones, and acorns. Have an adult help you cut a 2-foot (.61-m) twig from a tree branch. Pull all of the leaves and small shoots off the twig, so it's smooth. Paint the pinecones and acorns pink.

2. Cut a length of string about 2 feet (61 cm) long. Tie one end to the center of the twig. Glue the other end to a pinecone.

3. Glue two acorns onto the string. Space them evenly.

4. Cut two more 1 ½-foot (46-cm) lengths of string in a different color. Tie one on each side of the first string, about 3 inches (7.6 cm) apart. Glue a pinecone on the end and an acorn in the center of each string.

5. Cut two more lengths of a different color string about 1 foot (31 cm) long. Tie one on each side of the twig. Glue a pinecone to the end and an acorn to the center of each string.

Optional: Apply white glue to the pinecones and seedpods. Dip them into glitter to make them sparkle.

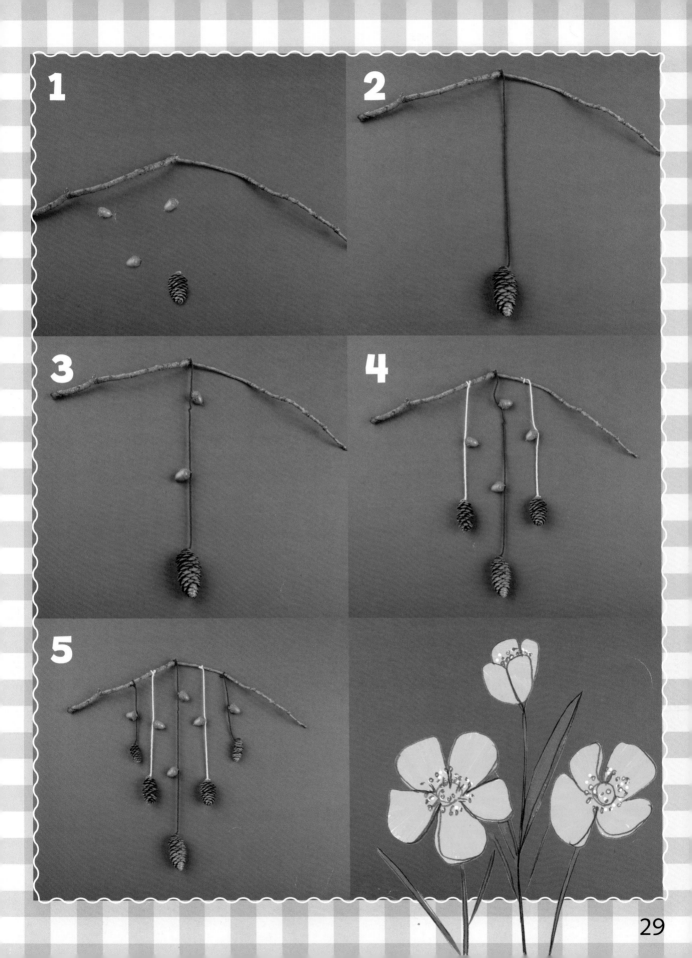

Spirit Stick

Spirit sticks are magical. Fill your stick with good thoughts and noisemakers. I like the tinkling sounds the bells make. My cousin Lucy likes beads best because they sound like rain.

You will need:

- paper towel tube
- brown tempera paint
- foam paintbrush
- black marker
- thin ribbon
- scissors
- white glue
- embroidery floss
- ruler
- bells
- tapestry needle
- beads

1. Paint the paper towel tube with brown paint. Let dry.

2. Add lines to the painted tube with marker to make the tube look like wood.

3. Cut two or three pieces of ribbon. Make them long enough to wrap around the tube. Wrap each ribbon around the tube, and glue in place.

4. Cut two full strands of embroidery floss, about 3 feet (.9 m) long. Tie one around each end of the tube using two knots. Squirt a thin line of glue along the looped part of each thread to hold it in place. Let dry.

5. String bells on the end of one strand using a tapestry needle.

6. Tie the ends of the string with a knot, and trim the thread. String beads onto the other strand. Tie a knot on the end of the string to secure.

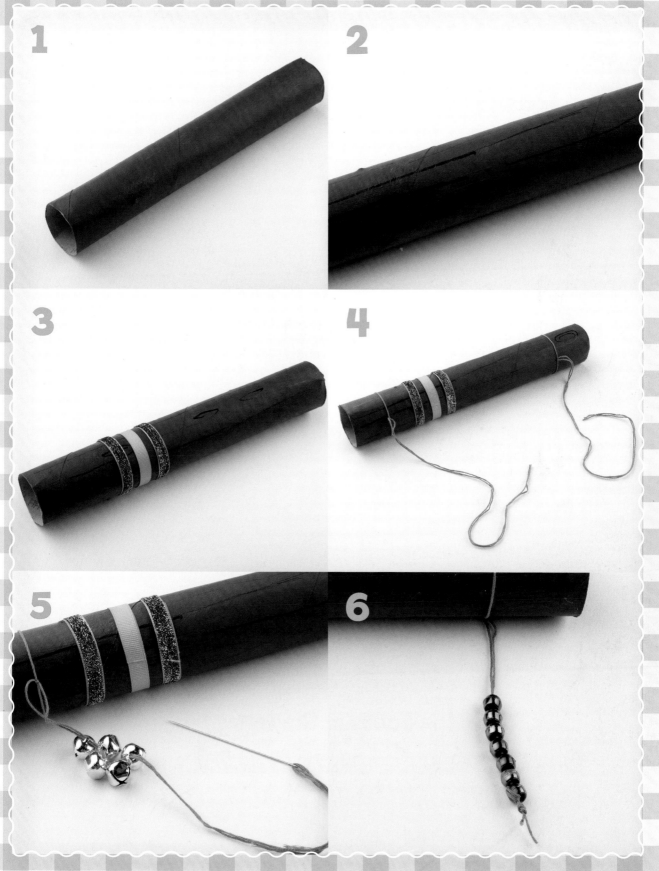

Read More

Peschke, Marci. *Summer Camp Queen.* Kylie Jean. North Mankato, Minn.: Picture Window Books, 2013.

Ross, Kathy. *Earth-Friendly Crafts: Clever Ways to Reuse Everyday Items.* Minneapolis: Millbrook Press, 2009.

Sirrine, Carol. *Cool Crafts with Old Jeans: Green Projects for Resourceful Kids.* Green Crafts. Mankato, Minn.: Capstone Press, 2010.

Internet Sites

FactHound offers a safe, fun way to find Internet sites related to this book. All of the sites on FactHound have been researched by our staff.

Here's all you do:

Visit *www.facthound.com*

Type in this code: 9781479521937

 Check out projects, games and lots more at
www.capstonekids.com

Look for all the books in the series:

Party Craft Queen   Rodeo Craft Queen

Pirate Craft Queen   Summer Camp Craft Queen